NATIONAL GEOGRAPHIC

D0100738

A Trip to the Doctor

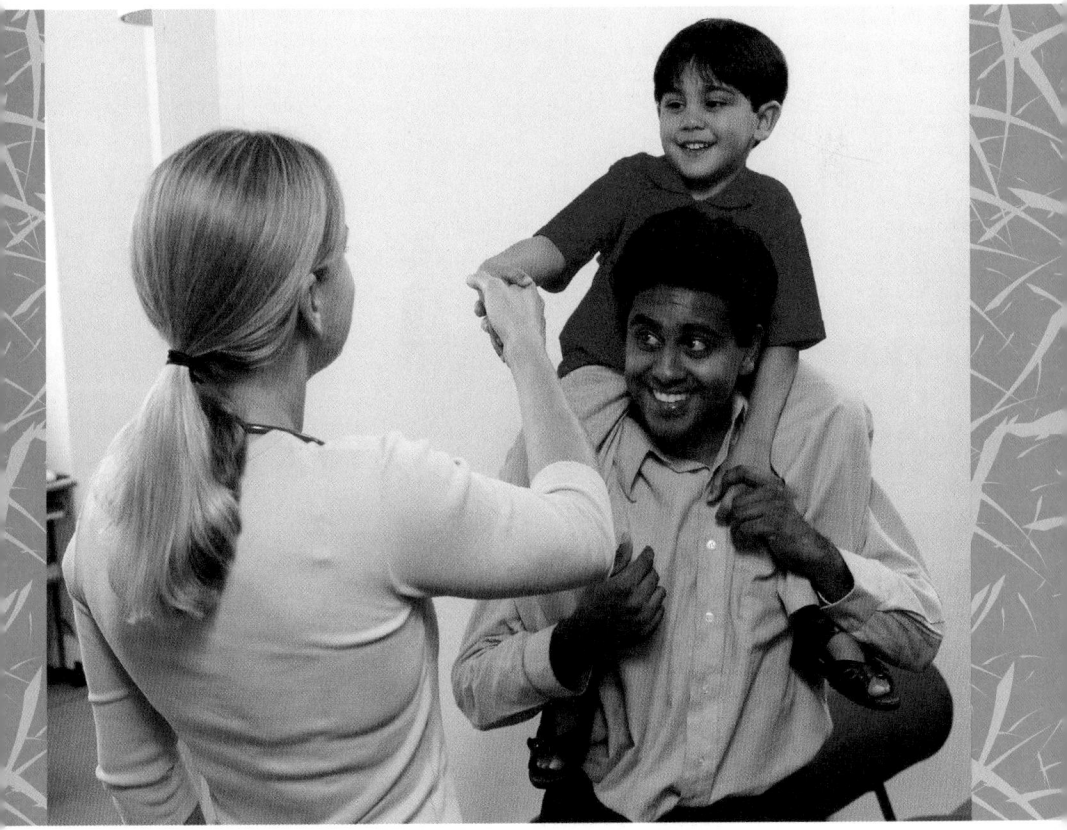

Jan Pritchett

My doctor takes care of me.

My doctor takes care of me.

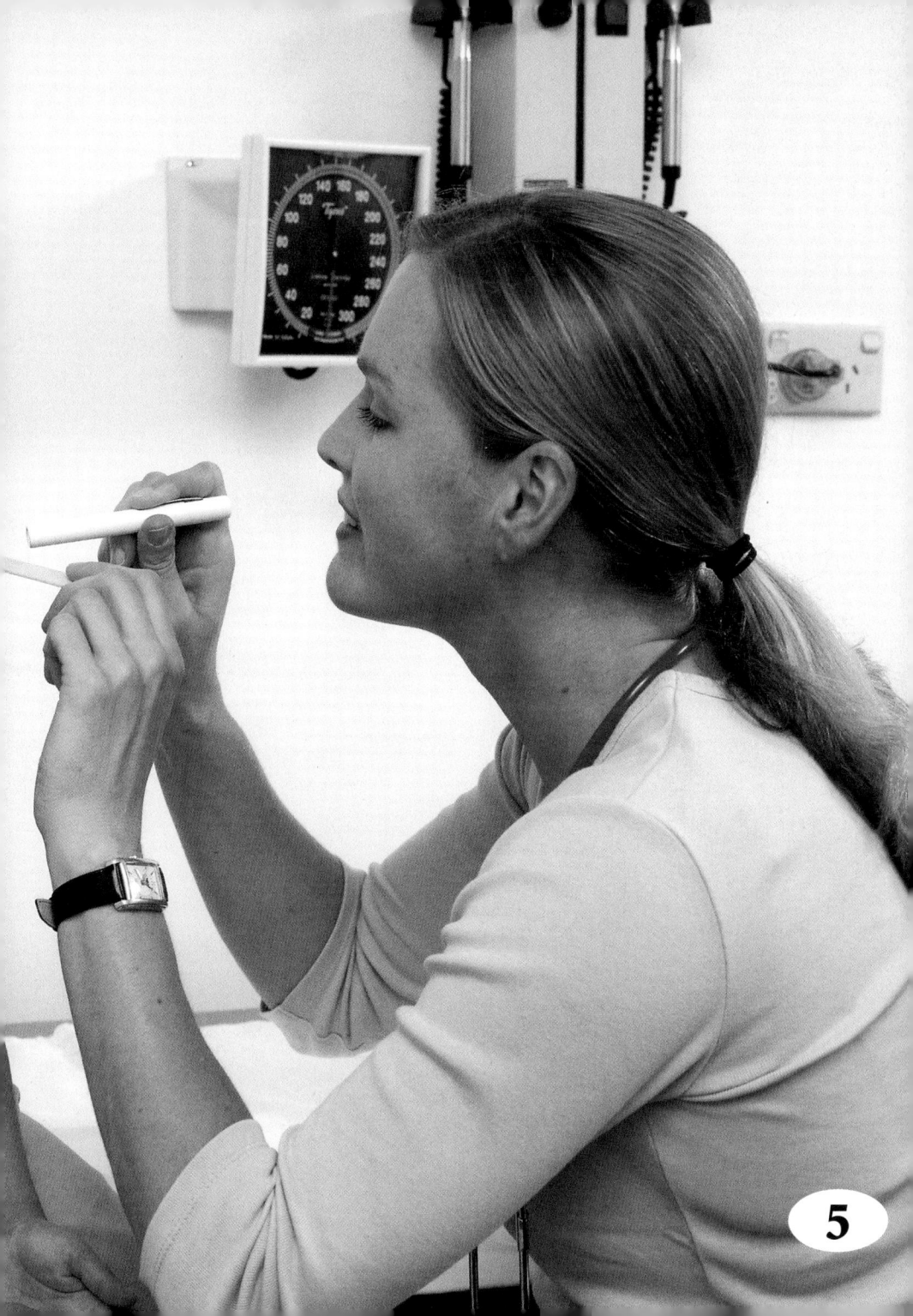

My doctor takes care of me.

My doctor takes care of me.

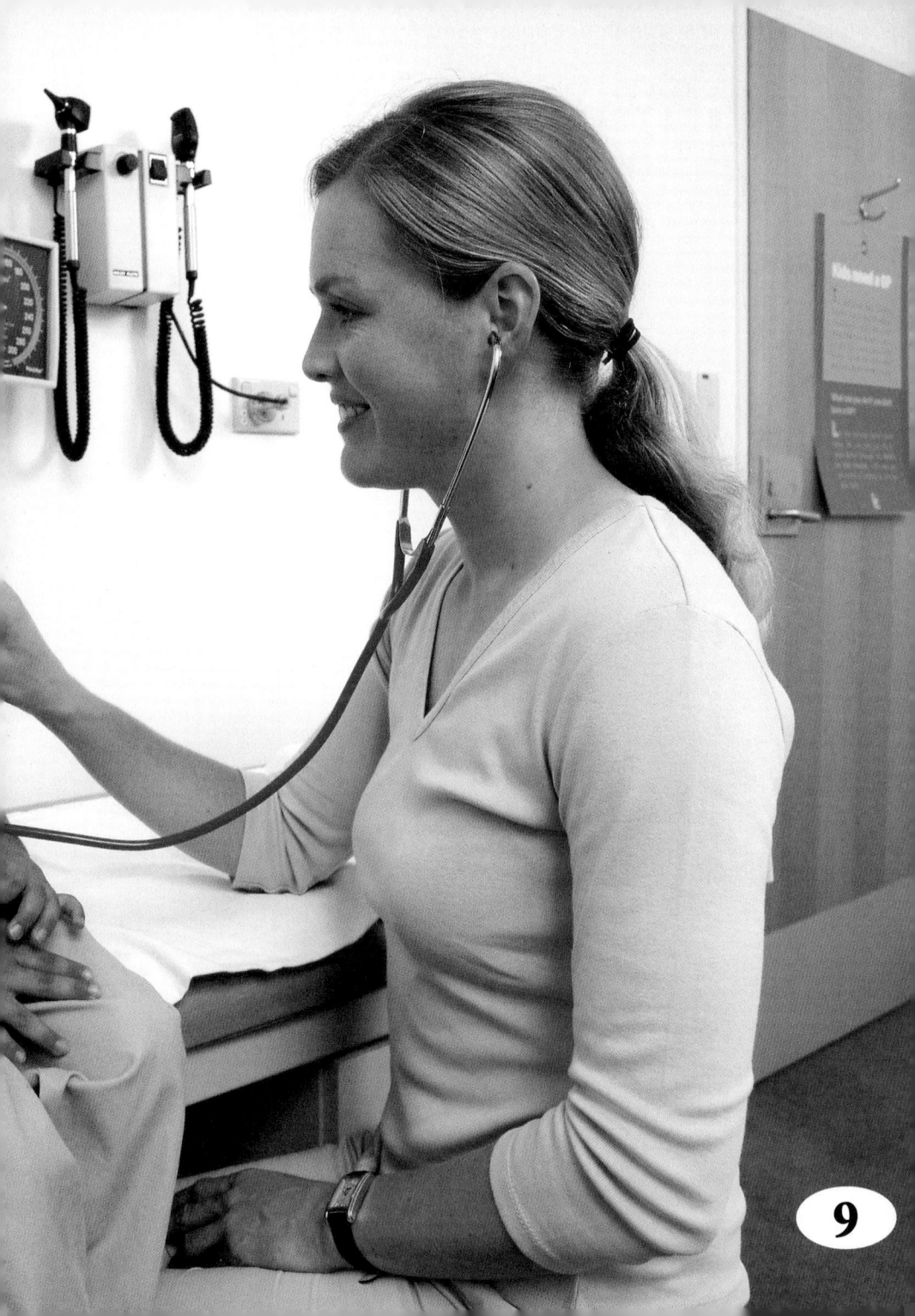

My doctor takes care of me.

My doctor takes care of me.